KATHRYN GIBBONS

Financial Freedom in Retirement

A Guide to Budgeting for Seniors on Fixed Incomes

This book was professionally typeset on Reedsy.
Find out more at reedsy.com

Contents

1

Introduction

Welcome to this new life season of retirement! If you are here, you have come to the right place for great information on how to plan for and thrive during your retirement years. Even if your income will be reduced, there are many ways you can stretch those reduced dollars and still be able to enjoy a full and satisfying life during this season.

This book aims to provide comprehensive guidance for retirees navigating the complexities of fixed incomes in retirement and will help you create an effective budget for financial stability and fulfillment.

Importance of budgeting for retirees on fixed incomes

Budgeting is crucial for retirees on fixed incomes as it helps in managing our finances effectively. With a fixed income, we often have limited financial resources, making it essential to allocate funds wisely to cover essential expenses such as housing, healthcare, food, utilities, and transportation.

Creating a budget allows us to plan for regular expenses, anticipate upcoming costs, and set aside funds for unexpected emergencies or healthcare needs. It also helps in controlling spending, avoiding debt, and ensuring that there's enough money for necessities throughout retirement.

Budgeting also enables retirees to explore potential ways to save money, take advantage of senior discounts or benefits, and make informed financial decisions to maintain our quality of life while living within our means.

Overview of challenges specific to fixed incomes in retirement

Retirement on a fixed income presents several challenges that can impact financial stability. Some areas that need to be considered are inflation, medical expenses, unforeseen emergencies or major expenses, and market fluctuations that can affect investments. We will get into these areas in more detail in the upcoming chapters, but all these things can leave retirees vulnerable. Balancing the desire for a comfortable retirement lifestyle with the limitations of a fixed income requires careful planning and budgeting to mitigate these challenges.

How effective budgeting can lead to financial stability and peace of mind

Effective budgeting plays a pivotal role in securing financial stability and fostering peace of mind. By diligently allocating resources, setting financial goals, and tracking expenditures, individuals can gain a clear understanding of their financial landscape. A Budget will:

- Offer a clear overview of income and expenses, enabling better financial organization and planning.
- Help prioritize essential expenses while cutting down on non-essential costs, ensuring our money is allocated where it matters most.
- Allow for setting aside funds for emergencies, which safeguards against financial burdens and offers a safety net.
- Help with setting financial goals, providing a roadmap to accomplish both short and long-term financial goals
- Reduce financial stress. Knowing where your money goes and having a plan in place alleviates stress and provides a sense of control and confidence.

During this new season budgeting takes on a new level of importance. A solid plan is needed to ensure that our fixed income stretches to cover the essentials like housing, healthcare, groceries, and all those must-haves. But it's not just about pinching pennies; it's about smart money management, taking advantage of senior discounts, planning for fun stuff, and being ready for any unexpected financial plot twists. Let's dig in and make sure this new life season is both comfortable and exciting!

2

Understanding Fixed Incomes in Retirement

Understanding fixed incomes in retirement involves grasping the array of sources available to provide a steady and predictable stream of funds during this life season.

Sources of fixed incomes

Retirees often rely on fixed income sources to sustain their lifestyle. Some common sources of fixed income for retirees include:

- **Social Security**: This is a government-administered program that provides a monthly income to retirees based on their earnings history.
- **Pensions**: Some retirees receive pensions from their employers, providing a fixed amount regularly after retirement.
- **Annuities**: These are financial products purchased from an insurance company, offering regular payments either for a specific period or for the rest of the retiree's life.
- **Bonds**: Retirees often invest in bonds, which pay regular interest

over a specified period, offering a predictable income stream.

- **Certificates of Deposit (CDs)**: CDs are low-risk investments offered by banks that pay a fixed interest rate over a specific period, providing a steady income.
- **Dividend-Paying Stocks**: Stocks from stable, dividend-paying companies can provide regular income through dividend payments.
- **Retirement Savings Withdrawals**: Retirees can withdraw money from their retirement savings accounts, such as 401(k)s or IRAs, which can provide a steady income stream if managed properly.

Diversifying across these sources can help retirees build a stable and reliable income stream during their retirement years.

Potential limitations and constraints of fixed income

Fixed income, while offering stability, comes with its limitations and constraints. Understanding these limitations is crucial in devising a comprehensive retirement income plan that considers the strategies to mitigate these risks:

- **Inflation Risk**: Fixed incomes may not keep pace with rising costs, leading to a decrease in purchasing power over time.
- **Vulnerability to Market Fluctuations**: Certain fixed-income investments can be impacted by market changes, affecting returns or jeopardizing the expected income stream.
- **Longevity Risk**: Outliving the income generated from fixed sources becomes a concern, particularly if these sources aren't designed to adjust for longer lifespans.
- **Lack of Flexibility**: Some fixed-income options have restrictions on withdrawals or penalties, limiting the ability to adapt to unexpected financial needs or changes in circumstances.

Planning for inflation and cost-of-living adjustments

The strategies listed below can help mitigate the impact of inflation and rising living costs on fixed incomes, helping to ensure a more sustainable financial plan for the long term.

- **Invest in Inflation-Protected Securities:** Consider investing in assets like Treasury Inflation-Protected Securities (TIPS) that adjust their value with inflation, offering protection against rising costs.
- **Diversify Income Sources:** Seek diverse income streams, including dividend-paying stocks, real estate investment trusts (REITs), or annuities with inflation riders, to hedge against inflation's impact on fixed incomes.
- **Regularly Review and Adjust:** Periodically review your budget and income sources to assess their alignment with rising living costs. Adjust spending patterns or consider alternative investments if needed.
- **Stay Informed and Flexible:** Keep an eye on economic trends and policy changes that might impact inflation. Being flexible and adaptable in financial planning allows for adjustments in response to changing circumstances or economic conditions.

Nailing down fixed incomes in retirement is key for financial stability later on. Social Security, pensions, bonds—they're the steady cash flow. But be aware of the downsides: inflation risks, market ups and downs, and the chance of outliving the cash. So, what's the solution? Mix up income sources, pick inflation-proof investments, and think about adjusting for rising costs. Flexibility and knowing your income sources inside out are the secrets to a solid retirement plan.

3

Assessing Expenses and Creating a Budget

Embarking on the journey of financial stability begins with a critical step: assessing expenses and crafting a well-defined budget. Understanding where money flows and how it's allocated is the cornerstone of sound financial management. This chapter delves into the art of evaluating expenses, developing a budget, and the impact this process has on shaping a secure financial future.

This detailed approach to assessing expenses and creating a budget will empower you to gain control over your finances, prioritize spending, and work towards achieving financial objectives. Regular review and adjustment ensure that your budget remains flexible and is aligned with evolving financial needs and goals.

Evaluate current spending

This process provides a clear picture of where money is being spent and highlights areas that might need adjustment.

- Take stock of expenses, categorize them, and understand where the money is going each month.

- Begin by tracking all expenses over a specific period, such as a month or several months. Categorize these expenses into groups like housing, utilities, groceries, transportation, entertainment, etc.

Identify Essential vs. Non-Essential Costs

Understanding this distinction helps prioritize spending and identify areas where cutbacks might be feasible.

- Distinguish between necessary expenses (like bills and groceries) and discretionary spending (like entertainment or dining out).
- Essential costs include items like rent or mortgage payments, utilities, groceries, insurance, and transportation for work.
- Non-essential costs are typically discretionary, including dining out, entertainment, subscription services, or shopping for non-essential items.

Set Realistic Financial Goals

§Define short-term and long-term financial objectives, aligning them with income and expenses.

- Short-term goals might involve building an emergency fund, paying off credit card debt, or saving for a vacation.
- Long-term goals could include retirement savings, buying a home, or investing for children's education.
- Ensure these goals are specific, measurable, achievable, relevant, and time-bound (SMART).

Allocate Funds Proactively

- Designate portions of income toward savings, emergency funds, debt repayment, and discretionary spending.
- Once expenses are categorized and financial goals are set, designate specific percentages or amounts of income toward essentials like bills and savings, and allocate a portion for discretionary spending.
- Prioritize debt repayment by allocating a portion of income towards paying off outstanding debts.

Track and Adjust Regularly

- Continuously monitor spending against your budget, making necessary adjustments to ensure financial goals are met.
- Use budgeting tools or apps to track spending and compare it with the set budget.
- Regularly review and adjust the budget as needed, especially when life changes occur, such as a change in income, unexpected expenses, or shifts in financial goals.

Sample Budget

Below is a list of items included in a typical budget. You can find free templates online that help with automating this information and they do all of the calculations for you. Feel free to customize the categories to align with your personal financial situation!

Monthly Income:
Pension: $XXXX
Social Security: $XXXX
Investment Income: $XXXX

Part-Time Work: $XXXX

Monthly Expenses:

Housing:
  Mortgage/Rent: $XXXX
  Property Taxes: $XXXX
  Home Insurance: $XXXX
  Utilities (Electricity, Gas, Water): $XXXX

Transportation:
  Car Payment/Insurance: $XXXX
  Gas/Fuel: $XXXX
  Public Transportation: $XXXX
  Food and Groceries: $XXXX

Healthcare:
  Health Insurance Premiums: $XXXX
  Prescription Medications: $XXXX
  Doctor Visits/Copays: $XXXX

Debt Payments:
  Credit Cards: $XXXX
  Loans (Personal, Student, etc.): $XXXX
  Entertainment/Leisure: $XXXX

Miscellaneous:
  Clothing: $XXXX
  Personal Care: $XXXX
  Subscriptions (Netflix, Gym, etc.): $XXXX
  Savings/Investments: $XXXX

Total Income: $XXXX

Total Expenses: $XXXX

Remaining Amount (Income - Expenses): $XXXX

Tips for Creating and Managing Your Budget:

Creating a sample budget provides a clear overview of your financial situation, allowing you to make informed decisions and manage your expenses effectively.

- **Track Your Spending**: Keep a record of every expense to understand where your money goes.
- **Differentiate Needs vs. Wants**: Prioritize essential expenses over discretionary spending.
- **Adjust and Review Regularly**: Periodically reassess and adjust your budget as circumstances change.
- **Emergency Fund**: Aim to build an emergency fund to cover unexpected expenses.
- **Seek Professional Advice**: Consider consulting a financial advisor for guidance and strategies specific to your situation.

The journey toward financial stability starts with understanding and managing expenses effectively. By evaluating spending habits, distinguishing between needs and wants, and crafting a budget that aligns with financial goals, individuals lay the groundwork for a more secure future. Regularly revisiting and adjusting this budget ensures flexibility and adaptability to life's changes while steering towards a path of financial well-being and peace of mind.

4

Housing Costs and Alternatives

ousing costs are by far the largest portion of any budget. Managing housing costs efficiently is crucial in ensuring financial stability and quality of life. This chapter focuses on strategic approaches to secure or maintain affordable housing options and leveraging available benefits and assistance programs to alleviate the financial burden associated with our number one expense.

Strategies for affordable housing options

Explore downsizing or relocating to a more affordable area to reduce housing expenses

- Assess space needs – Evaluate your current living space and determine if it aligns with your needs. If you find yourself with unused rooms or excessive square footage, downsizing to a smaller, more efficient space could lead to substantial cost savings.
- Financial benefits – Downsizing often translates to reduced mortgage or rent payments, property taxes, insurance costs, and utility expenses. Smaller spaces usually require less maintenance, leading

to further financial savings over time.

- Lifestyle considerations – Beyond financial aspects, downsizing can also simplify your lifestyle. It may foster a sense of freedom by reducing clutter and the responsibility of maintaining a larger property, allowing for more time and resources to pursue activities that bring joy.

Relocation considerations

- Research cost of living – Explore different regions or neighborhoods to identify areas with a lower cost of living. Consider factors like housing prices, property taxes, utility costs, and overall expenses specific to your lifestyle.
- Financial impact – Relocating to a more affordable area can dramatically reduce housing expenses. This shift might enable you to allocate more funds towards savings, investments, travel, or other personal interests.
- Community and amenities – While affordability is crucial, assess the community, amenities, healthcare facilities, and other essential services in the potential new location. Ensure it aligns with your lifestyle preferences and meets your needs.

Downsizing or relocating often involves adjusting to a new environment. Think about how this change might affect your daily life, social connections, and access to essential services.

Consider renting out a spare room. Renting out a spare room presents an opportunity to not only generate extra income but also create a mutually beneficial living arrangement. It's a chance to share your space, contribute to someone's housing needs, and potentially form meaningful connections—all while optimizing your finances and making the most of your home's resources.

- Benefits of renting out a spare room – it will provide an additional income stream. It will allow for sharing of expenses. In some places there are tax benefits associated with renting out a portion of your home.
- Considerations and preparations – you'll need to familiarize yourself with local rental laws, regulations and zoning requirements. Take time to carefully vet potential tenants to ensure compatibility and safety. Prepare the spare room for renting by ensuring it's clean, furnished (if necessary), and equipped with essential amenities
- Lifestyle adjustments – be prepared for adjustments in your lifestyle, including sharing common spaces and being mindful of each other's privacy. Maintain open communication with your tenant and be flexible and understanding in resolving any issues. Prioritize safety measures by ensuring locks, alarms, and safety protocols are in place.

Research government-subsidized housing programs or senior living communities that offer cost-effective housing options. A few programs you can research further are:

- Section 8 Housing Choice Voucher Program administered by the Department of Housing and Urban Development (HUD)
- Public Housing Program also administered by HUD
- Low-Income Housing Tax Credit (LIHTC) tax incentive program
- Housing for the Elderly (Section 202) and Housing for Persons with Disabilities (Section 811) – HUD programs that provide affordable housing options for elderly individuals (Section 202) and persons with disabilities (Section 811)
- Various programs and grants exist to aid individuals experiencing

homelessness or at risk of becoming homeless include the Continuum of Care (CoC) Program, and Emergency Solutions Grants (ESG), among others.

Evaluate the potential of a reverse mortgage as a source of income or to cover housing costs for eligible individuals. Reverse mortgages are financial products that enable homeowners aged 62 or older to convert a portion of their home equity into cash. Here's an overview of reverse mortgage options:

Home Equity Conversion Mortgage (HECM) – HECMs are the most common type of reverse mortgages and are insured by the Federal Housing Administration (FHA). Key features include:

- Payments to homeowners – borrowers can receive loan proceeds in various ways, such as a lump sum, monthly payments, line of credit or a combination of these options.
- Loan repayment is typically deferred until the homeowner sells the home, moves out, or passes away. At that point, the loan, along with accrued interest and fees, must be repaid, usually through the sale of the home
- Homeowners are still responsible for property taxes, insurance, and maintenance of the property and they must continue to live in the home as their primary residence.

Proprietary Reverse Mortgages– some financial institutions offer proprietary or private reverse mortgage options, which are not insured by the government but follow similar principles to HECMs:

- Higher loan amounts – Proprietary reverse mortgages may allow access to higher loan amounts than HECMs, especially for high-value homes.

- Eligibility requirements, interest rates, and fees may differ from HECMs. These loans are usually targeted at homeowners with high-value homes and specific financial profiles.

Single-Purpose Reverse Mortgages – These are typically offered by state or local government agencies or nonprofit organizations and are intended for specific purposes, such as property tax assistance or home repairs:

- These mortgages are designed for specific needs, such as home improvements, and may have restrictions on how loan proceeds can be used
- They often have lower upfront costs compared to HECMs or proprietary reverse mortgages but might offer a smaller loan amount.

Before considering a reverse mortgage, it's crucial to carefully evaluate the terms, fees, and implications. Speak with a HUD-approved counselor or financial advisor to understand the potential impact on your finances, home equity, and estate planning. Reverse mortgages can offer financial flexibility, but they also come with specific obligations and considerations that should be thoroughly understood before making a decision.

Effectively managing housing costs on a fixed income demands a proactive approach and strategic decision-making. By exploring affordable housing options, retirees can alleviate financial strain and ensure this critical need is met without compromising our overall financial stability. These strategies empower individuals to consider and navigate housing options with greater ease and confidence, for a more sustainable and fulfilling life in retirement.

5

Budgeting for Healthcare Expenses, Insurance, and Medications

Navigating healthcare expenses, insurance, and medication costs in retirement demands a well-structured budget and a clear understanding of the evolving healthcare landscape. Crafting a financial plan to cover medical needs becomes paramount as we transition into retirement. Accounting for healthcare costs, insurance premiums, and medication expenses ensures a stable and secure health-focused financial strategy for this phase of life.

Budgeting for Healthcare Expenses in Retirement:

- **Health Insurance Premiums**: Allocate funds for monthly premiums for Medicare, Medigap, or private insurance plans to ensure comprehensive coverage.
- Out-of-Pocket Costs: Account for deductibles, copayments, and coinsurance for medical services and prescription drugs.
- **Long-Term Care Planning**: Consider long-term care insurance or savings dedicated to potential assisted living or nursing care needs.

- **Routine Health Expenses**: Budget for routine check-ups, screenings, and preventive care, including dental and vision needs.

Managing Insurance Costs:

- **Understanding Medicare**: Learn about different Medicare plans (Parts A, B, C, and D) to choose the most suitable coverage for healthcare needs.
- **Supplemental Insurance (Medigap)**: Evaluate options for additional coverage to bridge gaps in Medicare and alleviate out-of-pocket expenses.
- **Medicaid Eligibility**: Explore Medicaid benefits and eligibility criteria for potential supplementary coverage.
- **Private Insurance**: Assess options for private health insurance, including coverage through employers or healthcare marketplaces, if applicable.

Budgeting for Medication Expenses:

- **Prescription Drug Coverage**: Estimate expenses for prescription drugs and consider Medicare Part D or supplemental plans that cover medications.
- **Generic Substitutions**: Discuss with healthcare providers the possibility of using generic medications to lower costs without compromising quality.
- **Mail-Order or Bulk Discounts**: Explore mail-order pharmacies or bulk purchase options for cost savings on maintenance medications.
- **Patient Assistance Programs**: Research programs offered by pharmaceutical companies or nonprofit organizations that provide financial aid for medications.

Budgeting for healthcare expenses, insurance, and medications in retirement is a crucial aspect of financial planning. By proactively allocating funds for medical needs, understanding insurance options, and exploring cost-saving measures for medications, individuals can create a comprehensive healthcare budget that ensures financial security and peace of mind throughout their retirement journey. A well-structured healthcare budget not only addresses current needs but also provides a safety net for unexpected healthcare costs, enabling retirees to embrace this phase of life with confidence and stability.

6

Maximizing Savings and Investments

In the pursuit of financial stability and growth, maximizing savings and investments is key for retirees on a fixed income. We need to learn how to make strategic choices, informed decisions, and develop an understanding of low-risk investment options. This strategy involves not only growing savings but also minimizing risks. Understanding the significance of diversification and adopting a long-term approach lays the groundwork for our financial future.

Overview of low-risk investment options suitable for fixed incomes

- **Bonds**: Bonds are debt securities where investors lend money to governments or corporations in return for periodic interest payments and the return of the principal amount at maturity. For those on fixed incomes, bonds serve as stable, income-generating assets. Government bonds, like U.S. Treasury bonds, are considered low-risk due to the backing of the government. Corporate bonds, while slightly riskier, can offer higher yields.
- **High-Yield Savings Accounts**: High-yield savings accounts typi-

cally offer interest rates higher than traditional savings accounts. They provide a safe avenue to park emergency funds or short-term savings while still earning a reasonable interest rate. These accounts often have FDIC insurance, ensuring protection for deposited funds up to a certain limit.

- **Certificates of Deposit (CDs)**: CDs offer fixed interest rates over a predetermined period, ranging from a few months to several years. They are FDIC-insured and provide a predictable return on investment, making them suitable for risk-averse investors. Early withdrawal might incur penalties, but they are an attractive option for those seeking stability and guaranteed returns.

Strategies for growing savings and minimizing risks

- **Dollar-Cost Averaging (DCA)**: DCA involves investing fixed amounts of money at regular intervals, regardless of market conditions. This strategy reduces the impact of market volatility by spreading out purchases over time. By consistently buying assets, investors may benefit from both low and high market cycles, potentially lowering the average cost per share over time.
- **Asset Allocation**: Asset allocation involves diversifying investments across different asset classes such as stocks, bonds, real estate, and commodities. This strategy aims to manage risk by not putting all eggs in one basket. Depending on risk tolerance and financial goals, adjusting the allocation can balance potential returns with risk exposure.
- **Robo-Advisors and Index Funds**: Robo-advisors offer automated investment management services, utilizing algorithms to create and manage portfolios based on an individual's risk tolerance and goals. They often offer low fees and diversified investment options. Index funds, which track a market index like the S&P 500, provide broad

market exposure with lower management fees compared to actively managed funds.

Importance of diversification and long-term planning

- **Diversification**: Diversification is the practice of spreading investments across different asset classes, industries, and geographic regions. It helps reduce the impact of a decline in any single investment, minimizing potential losses. A diversified portfolio aims to balance risk and return by not relying heavily on any single asset or sector.
- **Long-Term Planning**: Long-term planning involves setting clear financial goals and developing strategies to achieve them over an extended period. It involves disciplined investing, focusing on the power of compounding returns over time. By staying invested through market fluctuations, individuals can potentially benefit from the market's upward trajectory.

Maximizing savings and investments while on a fixed income requires a balance between risk management and growth opportunities. Choosing low-risk investment options tailored for fixed incomes, adopting prudent strategies, and embracing diversification while focusing on the long-term goal is key. This journey toward financial stability demands adaptability, informed choices, and a commitment to the long-haul vision—a vision where a diversified portfolio, strategic planning, and informed decisions pave the way toward a secure financial future.

7

Lifestyle Adjustments and Frugal Living Tips

Retirement, and a transition to a fixed income, may require adjustments to our lifestyle to harmonize with our new financial realities. It becomes important to embrace frugality and make thoughtful adjustments to ensure financial stability without sacrificing quality of life. By navigating prudent spending, embracing community resources, and discovering cost-effective activities, retirees can make the most of their fixed income and enjoy a full life.

Adapting lifestyle to match fixed income realities

- **Budgeting and Prioritizing Expenses**: As noted in Chapter 3, crafting a detailed budget tailored to the fixed income sets the tone for financial stability. Prioritize essential expenses like housing, utilities, and healthcare while scrutinizing discretionary spending. Being mindful of non-essential costs helps align expenditures with income constraints.
- **Downsizing and Simplifying**: Consider downsizing living arrangements or possessions to reduce maintenance and utility

costs. Embracing a simpler lifestyle not only saves money but also simplifies daily routines, fostering a sense of ease and freedom.

- **Reviewing Subscriptions and Services**: Assess subscriptions, memberships, or services that may no longer align with current needs. Cancel or renegotiate contracts to eliminate unnecessary expenses, ensuring that each dollar spent contributes meaningfully to life's essentials.

Tips for reducing expenses without compromising quality of life

- **Meal Planning and Smart Shopping**: Plan meals ahead, embrace home cooking, and shop strategically by using grocery lists and seeking discounts or coupons. This practice not only cuts food costs but also encourages healthier eating habits.
- **Energy and Utility Efficiency**: Implement energy-saving habits like using energy-efficient appliances, unplugging electronics when not in use, and optimizing heating and cooling systems. Simple changes can significantly reduce utility bills without compromising comfort.
- **DIY and Repurposing**: Explore do-it-yourself solutions and repurposing items to minimize expenses. Engaging in DIY projects or finding new uses for existing items can reduce the need for purchasing new things.

Engaging in community resources and free/low-cost activities

- **Senior Discounts and Programs**: Take advantage of senior discounts offered by various establishments, including restaurants, theaters, and stores. Additionally, explore local senior centers or community programs that provide low-cost or free activities tailored for retirees.
- **Volunteer Opportunities**: Engaging in volunteer work not only contributes to the community but also offers social connections and the chance to participate in activities without financial obligations. Volunteering for local events or organizations can provide a sense of purpose and fulfillment.
- **Utilizing Public Spaces and Events**: Leverage public parks, libraries, and community centers for free or low-cost recreational activities, educational programs, or cultural events. These spaces often offer a wealth of resources and opportunities for social engagement.

Navigating retirement on a fixed income necessitates a deliberate blend of financial prudence and resourcefulness. We need to adapt lifestyle choices to align with income realities, seek innovative ways to trim expenses without compromising satisfaction, and tap into community resources. By embracing frugality and finding value in both the simple pleasures and communal offerings, retirees can forge a fulfilling path, ensuring financial stability while savoring a rich and meaningful post-career season in life.

8

Psychological and Emotional Aspects of Budgeting in Retirement

Entering this new season of retirement can be exciting and stressful at the same time and can often trigger psychological and emotional responses. The art of budgeting in retirement goes beyond numbers, touching the deeper realms of mental health and emotional well-being. Coping with financial stress, nurturing mental resilience, and discovering purpose amid budgetary constraints are all part of navigating the psychological and emotional landscape of retirement finances.

Coping with financial stress and anxiety

- **Open Communication**: Establish open dialogues with loved ones or financial advisors to address concerns and devise strategies. Sharing worries and seeking guidance often alleviates the burden of financial stress and promotes a sense of support.
- **Mindfulness and Stress Management**: Embrace mindfulness practices like meditation, deep breathing exercises, or yoga to manage stress and anxiety. These techniques help foster a sense of

calmness and clarity amidst financial uncertainties.

- **Seeking Professional Support**: Consider seeking assistance from financial counselors or therapists specializing in financial therapy. Professional guidance can aid in reframing perspectives and developing coping mechanisms to manage financial-related stressors.

Strategies for maintaining mental health and well-being

- **Engaging in Hobbies and Activities**: Dedicate time to hobbies, interests, or activities that bring joy and fulfillment without significant financial outlays. Engaging in creative pursuits or hobbies fosters a sense of purpose and provides avenues for relaxation and self-expression.
- **Establishing Routine and Structure**: Create a daily routine that incorporates mental and physical wellness practices, such as exercise, social interactions, and relaxation techniques. Having a structured routine can provide stability and a sense of control amid financial uncertainties.
- **Cultivating Social Connections**: Prioritize social connections by staying connected with friends, family, or joining community groups. Strong social ties serve as a vital support system, offering emotional resilience and companionship during challenging financial phases.

Finding purpose and fulfillment in retirement within budgetary constraints

- **Exploring Volunteer Opportunities**: Engage in volunteer work aligned with personal interests or causes. Volunteering not only contributes positively to society but also provides a sense of purpose and fulfillment, irrespective of financial limitations.
- **Pursuing Lifelong Learning**: Embrace opportunities for continuous learning, whether through online courses, workshops, or local educational programs. Cultivating new skills or knowledge enriches personal growth and can instill a sense of accomplishment.
- **Embracing Personal Passions**: Revisit and embrace personal passions or long-held aspirations. Whether it's starting a small business, pursuing a hobby more seriously, or contributing to a cause, aligning actions with passions can infuse life with meaning and fulfillment.

The psychological and emotional facets of budgeting in retirement underscore the need for a holistic approach that encompasses mental well-being alongside financial considerations. By nurturing mental resilience, fostering purpose, and seeking fulfillment within budgetary constraints, retirees can chart a path towards a more emotionally fulfilling and psychologically balanced retirement journey. Beyond the numbers, lies the opportunity to cultivate resilience, find purpose, and embrace a fulfilling retirement anchored in emotional well-being.

9

Conclusion: Embracing Financial Freedom in Retirement

The pursuit of financial freedom in retirement is a journey marked by wisdom, resilience, and the courage to adapt to new realities. As seniors navigate fixed incomes, the essence lies not only in managing resources but in embracing a mindset that fosters stability and contentment. Summarizing key takeaways and actionable steps paves the way for a more secure financial future, offering encouragement and motivation for those charting their course through this unique phase of life.

Summarizing key takeaways and actionable steps

- **Budgeting and Prioritization**: Crafting a detailed budget aligned with fixed incomes and prioritizing essential expenses form the bedrock of financial stability. Regularly revisiting and adjusting the budget ensures adaptability to changing circumstances.
- **Diversification and Prudent Investments**: Embracing diversification across various low-risk investment options helps mitigate risks and maximize returns. Utilizing strategies like dollar-cost

averaging and seeking professional advice facilitates informed investment decisions.

- **Lifestyle Adjustments and Resourcefulness**: Adapting to a simpler lifestyle, reducing expenses without compromising quality of life, and leveraging community resources and low-cost activities contribute significantly to financial well-being.

Encouragement and motivation for seniors navigating fixed incomes

- **Resilience Amid Challenges**: Each financial hurdle presents an opportunity for growth and resilience. Embracing challenges as opportunities to learn and adapt empowers individuals to navigate fixed incomes with confidence.
- **Celebrating Small Wins**: Acknowledge and celebrate milestones achieved in the journey towards financial stability. Every step taken, no matter how small, contributes to the broader goal of financial freedom.
- **Seeking Support and Guidance**: Never hesitate to seek support, whether from financial advisors, community resources, or loved ones. Support networks offer invaluable guidance and emotional reinforcement.

Final thoughts on achieving financial stability and enjoying retirement

- **Embracing the Journey**: Remember, achieving financial stability in retirement is not solely about reaching a destination but savoring the journey itself. Each decision made, every adjustment, contributes to a more fulfilling and secure retirement.
- **Prioritizing Well-being**: Amidst financial pursuits, prioritize mental and emotional well-being. A balanced life, filled with purpose, joy, and meaningful connections, is the true essence of a successful retirement.

As you enter this new season in your life, I hope you can enjoy financial freedom as it intertwines with new experiences, learnings, and growth. This journey leads not only to financial stability but to a life rich in contentment and fulfillment. With each prudent financial choice along with a mindful approach to retirement, the path becomes clearer, paving the way for a fulfilling and secure chapter that is uniquely your own. Ultimately, the pursuit of financial freedom in retirement is not merely about the numbers but about embracing a life lived on your own terms, embracing newfound freedoms, and cherishing the true wealth found in every moment.

If you found this book helpful, I'd be very appreciative if you left a favorable review for the book on Amazon!

10

Resources

Resources:

Kline, B. (2023, December 22). 10 Budget Templates & Tools That Will Change Your Life. *The Savvy Mama*. https://thesavvymama.com/budget-templates/#:~:text=Google%20Sheets%20has%20plenty%20of,will%20be%20perfect%20for%20you

Housing Choice Voucher Program Section 8. (2022, January 11). HUD.gov / U.S. Department of Housing And Urban Development (HUD). https://www.hud.gov/topics/housing_choice_voucher_program_section_8

HUD's public housing program. (2021, October 28). HUD.gov / U.S. Department of Housing And Urban Development (HUD). https://www.hud.gov/topics/rental_assistance/phprog

Low-Income Housing Tax Credit (LIHTC) | HUD USER. (n.d.). https://www.huduser.gov/portal/datasets/lihtc.html

Multifamily Housing - Program Description: Section 202 Supportive. (n.d.).

HUD.gov / U.S. Department of Housing And Urban Development (HUD). https://www.hud.gov/program_offices/housing/mfh/progd esc/eld202

Multifamily Housing - Program Description. (n.d.). HUD.gov / U.S. Department of Housing And Urban Development (HUD). https://w ww.hud.gov/program_offices/housing/mfh/progdesc/disab811

Continuum of Care program. (n.d.). HUD.gov / U.S. Department of Housing And Urban Development (HUD). https://www.hud.gov/prog ram_offices/comm_planning/coc

Emergency Solutions Grants Program. (n.d.). https://www.hudexchange. info/programs/esg/

HUD FHA Reverse Mortgage for Seniors (HECM). (n.d.). HUD.gov / U.S. Department of Housing And Urban Development (HUD). https://ww w.hud.gov/program_offices/housing/sfh/hecm/hecmhome

Folger, J. (2022, May 9). *Who needs a proprietary reverse mortgage?* Investopedia. https://www.investopedia.com/mortgage/reverse-mor tgage/proprietary/

Kagan, J. (2021, September 8). *Single-Purpose Reverse Mortgage: What It is, How It Works.* Investopedia. https://www.investopedia.com/terms/ s/singlepurpose-reverse-mortgage.asp

9 798887 263509